ABOUT FACE

ABOUT FACE
PORTRAITS AT UNION THEOLOGICAL SEMINARY

AN ARTIST'S BOOK BY CATHY BUSBY

Institute for Art, Religion, & Social Justice
Union Theological Seminary
Printed Matter, Inc.

About Face: Portraits at Union Theological Seminary
Cathy Busby

The artist completed this project during a residency
at The Institute for Art, Religion, & Social Justice,
January – May, 2012.

© 2012 The Institute for Art, Religion, & Social Justice and Cathy Busby

Design: Emily Davidson
Photography: Tanya Busse and Cathy Busby
Research Assistance: Kim Parkhill
Intern: Ted Kerr
Printing: Shapco Printing, Minneapolis

First edition, 2012

ISBN: 978-0-89439-061-6

The Institute for
Art, Religion, & Social Justice

The Institute for Art, Religion, & Social Justice
Union Theological Seminary in the City of New York
artreligionandsocialjustice.org

Printed Matter, Inc.

Printed Matter, Inc.
www.printedmatter.org

In memory of my father
E. David Busby (1928-1994)
who graduated from Union in 1957

PREFACE

AA Bronson

Co-Director, The Institute for Art, Religion, & Social Justice

I am at my computer in the early morning light, here in Amsterdam, where I have come to speak at a conference that addresses a quotation from Foucault: "I find it surprising that in our society art has become something that only refers to objects and not to individuals and their lives." It seems appropriate to write this short text here: what better context in which to address the formal portraits that occupy the halls of Union Theological Seminary, now reduced to ghosts, their meanings lost, the names of the subjects lost, their physical selves abused, many relegated to closets and storage rooms, undocumented, unloved. No longer do these artworks refer to beloved individuals and their lives.

Why was each portrait commissioned? Sometimes to stroke the ego of a donor, but more often to mark the departure of a great human being. These paintings were intended to honor their subjects, and yet the format of the academic portrait leaves them curiously cold and without affect. These are not portraits of great fighters, caught in their battle for human freedom; nor do they capture the other-worldliness of the spiritual mystic; nor the passion of the public intellectual. They survive as icons of white male power, depicted in a manner devised for the portrayal of kings and princes, now used for figures of academic prestige.

If inspiration was intended, where are we to find it? How were these paintings commissioned? How was the artist chosen? With what mission was the artist charged?

The subjects are mostly seated; the favored props are the academic gown and a book. The more recent subjects wear white shirts and ties, even the single portrait of a worker of color (Charles Henry). Although Union is noted for a focus on social justice, no image here openly refers to social action: the civil rights movement is not represented. Neither is the liberation of women. There is nothing that suggests that Union was a birthplace for feminist theology, womanist theology, black liberation theology, queer theology. Theology itself is reduced to a gown, to a book.

The presentation of love and of grace is not an easy proposition. One fears it has not been a proposition at all in the history of portraiture at Union. Only in one of the earliest portraits, that of Thomas McAuley (1778–1862) painted by Daniel P. Huntington, do we find in the modest size, and the attention to detail, a loving portrait. Perhaps I am too demanding; and yet the history of portraiture, and especially the history of religious portraiture, suggests that great paintings inspire.

While writing this text, I find myself imagining: what painter would I choose? And who would I choose to represent, and why? And where would I want this portrait to hang? And who would I want to be its caretaker? And how would I want it treated on a daily basis?

I imagine a narrative like this: the Union Refectory is emptied of portraits and ten new portraits are commissioned, portraits of its most prominent black educators over the last 175 years, all by black artists, all to be hung in this room. Collectively, the portraits tell a story: what is the story of African-American experience at Union?

Or this: the Union Social Hall is emptied of portraits and ten new portraits are commissioned, portraits of women in the history of Union, all by women artists, all to be hung in this room. What is the collective history of Union that these paintings tell?

Or this: the existing portraits are searched out, collected and documented. The artist, Cathy Busby, makes of them a living artwork, collecting stories, determining identities, knitting together a history that these paintings describe, not the expected story of important men, but a story of disruptions, upsets, and omissions. That story becomes itself a kind of historical portrait, and that portrait is painted in the form of this very book, the book you hold now in your hands.

March 13, 2012

PORTRAIT PROJECT: AN INTRODUCTION

Cathy Busby

When I first came to Union Theological Seminary as one of the artists in the exhibition *Art & Social Justice* in the Fall of 2010, I noticed the painted portraits in the Social Hall and the Refectory. At a glance, many appeared to be nineteenth century, in poor condition and a little crooked on the walls. This seemed peculiar, running counter to the general sense of architectural grandeur of Union. When I returned home to Halifax, I asked AA Bronson and Kathryn Reklis, Co-Directors of the Institute of Art, Religion, & Social Justice, if they would be interested in a proposal for an artist-in-residence to work with these portraits, to reposition them physically and in discourse. It so happened that my inquiry coincided with the 175th anniversary celebrations of the institution and seemed to dovetail nicely with the ideas being discussed for marking this occasion. Over a period of a year, we put plans into place and I began work at Union in January 2012.

It turned out that there were many more portraits than those I had seen on the walls and they were in various storage rooms, closets, and elsewhere. I found two in the wings of the Social Hall stage crowded by bags of linens and casually stored music stands. The actual hands-on work of finding, photographing and systematically documenting the portraits became a necessary part of the project. Early on, Ruth Tonkiss Cameron, Archivist, was able to provide three lists that included the portraits; one list from 1951, and two lists from 1966, one of which was revised in 1973. Through a combination of speaking with people and looking around, I was able to locate sixty-three that you see pictured on the following pages. There were some that we couldn't find, up to thirteen in all, and some that we couldn't identify. These are listed at the end of the catalog in the final section of this book.

...things as they are...re-thinking the portraits...

In my practice I work with things as they are. And though I care about the portraits as artworks and historical documents, I'm not recommending their restoration. I realize there's a randomness to them with many important figures in the institution's history not represented. And yet they provide a sampling of American institutional portrait painting. Among the twenty-six identified artists are Daniel P. Huntington, Margery A. Ryerson, Hubert Vos, Alice Boscowitz, J. W. L. Forster, Elmer Wesley Green and Everett Raymond Kinstler.

I'm interested in traces of institutional history and I often assemble or work with existing collections. For example, as artist-in-residence at the Art Gallery of Nova Scotia, for my installation, *Atrium* (2010), I gathered all the works that made reference to First Nations' cultures and assembled them as a collection. Then I reproduced their silhouettes on under-used walls at the entrance to the Gallery.

Union is a popular film and TV set location providing a valued income stream for the institution. My first experience of one of the film crews was one day when I was heading to the Administration hall on the first floor. I saw a large portrait leaning against a wall that I hadn't seen before. For a few seconds I wondered how I could have missed it until now. Then I realized it was a fake, a prop. It belonged to the set dressers. When I looked closely I could see that it was a digital print on canvas with some added surface texture.

Later that day I had a call from Michael Orzechowski in Facilities asking if I'd supervise the take down of portraits in the Refectory for this film shoot. I had always seen those portraits, the real ones that are fragile and heavy, as literally out of reach, but for this film crew they were just more things that had to be moved out of the way: a ladder, a strong guy, an assistant on the ground, some bubble wrap. That was it. But I know that handling actual artwork is risky. This time we were lucky.

At Union the portraits represent the subjects themselves, like Francis Brown over the fireplace in the Social Hall, as well as a variety of institutional memory lapses and unfinished actions. If a portrait is taken down, where will it be stored? While they were originally commissioned with an understanding of a permanent recognition of the subject ensconced in history, now many are in a deteriorated state. In fact, paintings are relatively fragile and impermanent, especially if met with inattention. The holes, tears and scores highlight their vulnerability. In a major museum such objects would receive professional attention and protection. At Union they mingle with daily life.

THE
PORTRAITS

The following images of Union's sixty-three portraits are in chronological order, concluding with five that are unidentified. The Catalog in the final section of the book provides details of these portraits.

REVEREND HENRY WHITE, D.D.

REVEREND SAMUEL WASHBURN
FOR WHOM
THE ORDER OF CHURCH HISTORY
IS NAMED

FISHER HOWE
DIRECTOR 1856-1871

SAMUEL HANSON COX

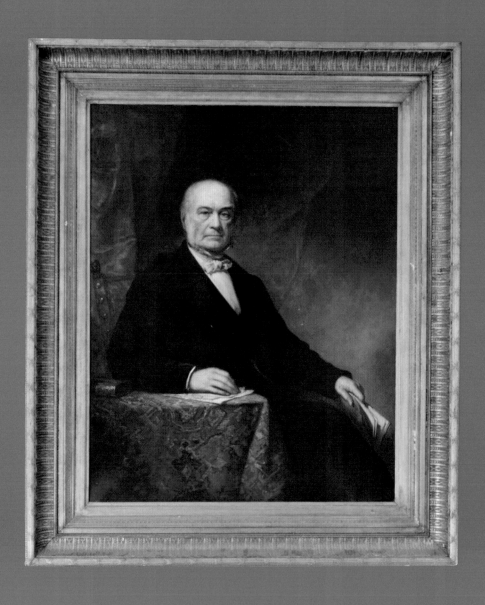

REVEREND HENRY B. SMITH, D.D., LL.D.

SAMUEL MILES HOPKINS, D.D.
Ecclesiastical History and Church Polity
1847 — 1901

Reverend John Hopkins Worcester, D.D.
PROFESSOR of SYSTEMATIC THEOLOGY 1877-1893

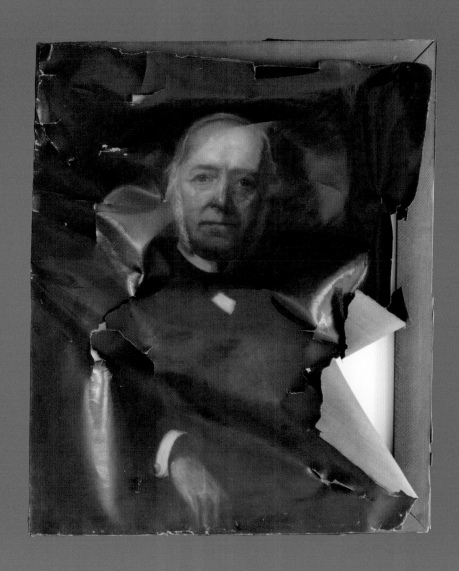

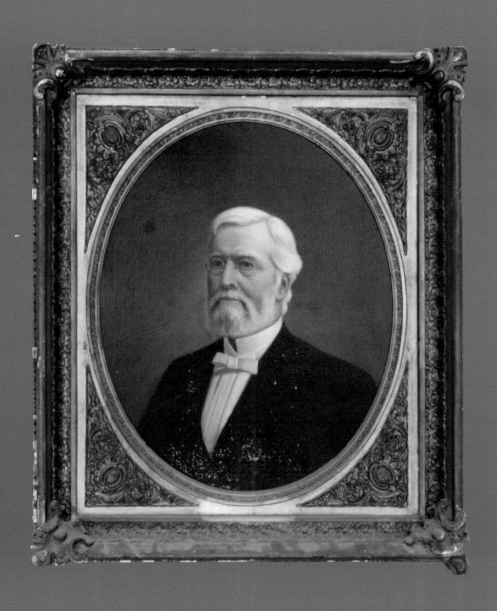

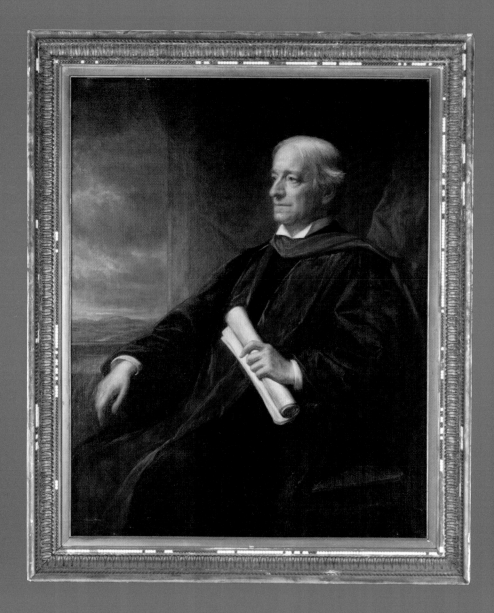

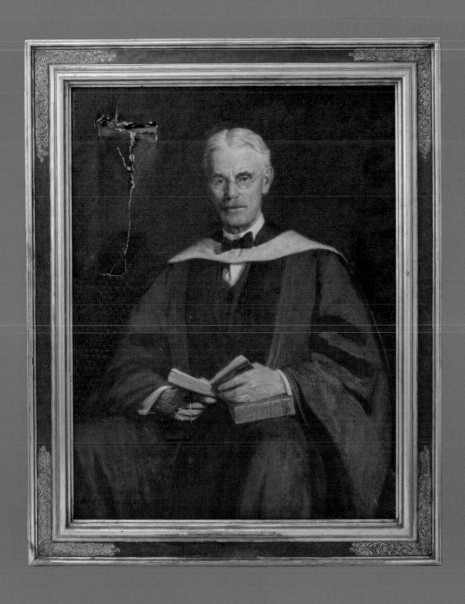

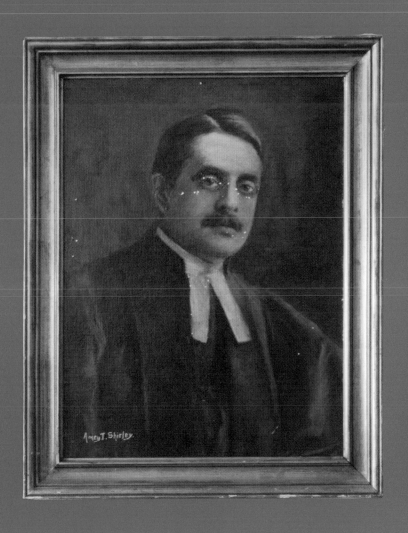

HELENA ADELL DICKINSON, M.A., Ph.D., Mus.D.
1875 - 1957

LECTURER SCHOOL OF SACRED MUSIC
1928 - 1945

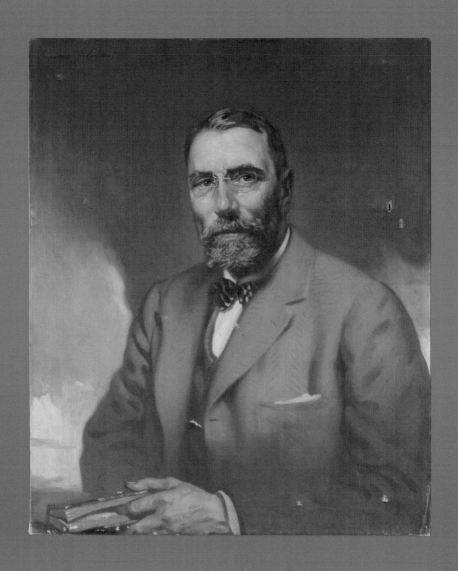

HAROLD H. TRYON UTS 1905
MEMBER OF THE UNION FACULTY 1908 - 1947
REGISTRAR 1924 - 1944
SECRETARY OF THE FACULTY 1929 - 1944

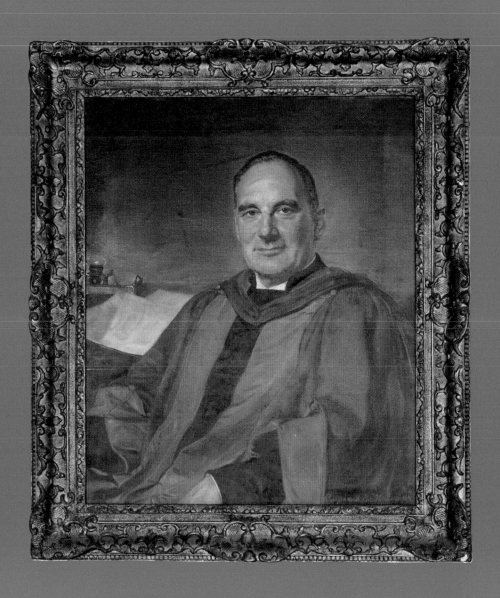

ROSALIND EVERDELL HANSMEYER
DIRECTOR 1960–1980
CHAIR, BOARD OF DIRECTORS 1975–1977

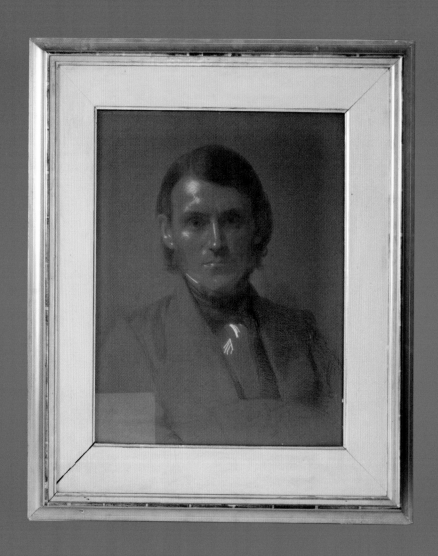

MULTIPLE VOICES

PORTRAIT STORIES AT UNION
JANUARY–MARCH 2012

The following contributions began as casual conversations and reflections evoked by the portraits and my interest in them. I formalized the process slightly by approaching a number of people from the Union community, asking them to share their views, memories and feelings about the portraits.

The Gaze...

Rev. Stephanie A. Duzant, MSW; MDiv candidate 2012:
Walls in Halls where Social Refectory gatherings take place
Speak to me with gazes intentionally placed in portrait-ed stares
Glaring at my Womanist essence with a look that reminds me...
That in spite of all the theological birthing that turned baskets
Filled with theses and dissertations put on academic rivers
By brave Mothers who are now mighty midwives
To those of us called to carry the soul of Womanism
At Union, into the new Millennium...
That they...the ghosts of the white men whose social justice stand
Lacked the liberation that all students needed...are still here
And the spiritual reason to correct the academic deficiency still exists.

"...imagining them as real people..."

Callie Janoff, MDiv student: "I've always seen that the portraits were here, but I've never really looked carefully at them. With knowing about your project, I've been seeing them in a new way. I find myself spending contemplative time with them, imagining them as real people who lived and worked here, who had their own smells and textures of skin and bodies that breathed and mouths that spoke."

"...where the portrait was hanging..."

Phyllis Conley, Development, 1961-2002: "There were many times when I'd get a call from the President's office, 'Phyllis, there are people in the office visiting NYC and they'd like to see the portrait that a member of their family donated to the Seminary. Can you take them around?' I usually got the call because of my longevity and so it was automatically assumed that I would know where the portrait was hanging. With much trepidation, I would take them to where I thought it was and I would usually find a blank wall. I would have to make up a story and say that the portraits were moved around and a committee had been formed to decide the best place to hang them. Then I had to try and locate the portrait, which was a fun job. It was a great day for Union when Katharine Shinn was commissioned to do the 1966 *Alphabetical and Location Listings of Plaques, Paintings, and Memorials* of the donated holdings and portraits, which she revised in 1973."

"…He was arrested on the lawn of the White House?"

Kim Parkhill, theatre artist / research assistant: "In the early weeks of the project, we were surrounded by portraits collected for safekeeping in the Institute of Art, Religion, & Social Justice office. There they were, staring at us, like characters in a drama I had yet to understand. So, I dubbed them our 'friends.' Some were wrapped in translucent paper; these became 'ghost friends.'

The portraits are inert art objects, remnants of a passing tradition, unseen or forgotten except for their faults: their condition, their inconvenience, their misrepresentation or under-representation of present day reality. The search for the subjects' identity was weirdly exciting; Googling a name from the 1951 Listing could result in a definitive photo match with one of the mystery 'friends,' or an interesting biography of the subject or artist. I felt such satisfaction when the detective work was rewarded with a positive finding. They re-animated when we discovered the names and details of the subjects' lives, prompting discussion, debate and exclamations like: 'You don't say! He was arrested on the lawn of the White House?' [former Union President John C. Bennett] or 'That guy is President Roosevelt's great-grandfather? No kidding!'

My mind is never far from the theatre, so I can't help but see the stories of the portraits, the institution,

Portrait found in Social Hall storage, January 2012

and the real people in them through that lens. There's metaphor and mystery, multiple plotlines, protagonists and antagonists (depending on the narrator), and conflicting perspectives leading to dramatic tension."

May 1969

Ron Grimes, alumnus: In 1968, there were many building occupations by students protesting the war in Vietnam. The next year at Union there were occupations of James Chapel and the Social Hall. During one of these, we took down some of presidential portraits, turning their faces to the wall, a symbolic way of calling into question the governance of the institution, just as we were questioning the governance of the country. The *New York Times*, describing the Union occupation, noted that Union students had 'put the doilies back on the tables' as they left. If there were, in fact, doilies, I

don't remember them, but the point was that, although dissident, we were respectful (or maybe just quaint). In response to persistent lobbying, some student representatives were for a brief time included in a few governance decisions. I was among those students and have a vivid memory of walking through the quadrangle with John Bennett, then president, as he worried aloud that such direct involvement of students in decision-making threatened the viability of the institution. I tried to comfort him by teasing, 'John, come on, we put the doilies back.' Probably not much comforted, he nevertheless laughed. Forty-odd years later, what do I think? Where are the women on the walls? If there isn't one already, there should be a portrait of John's wife Anne on some prominent Union wall. She, after all, had been active among us as a protester. In fact, if I recall correctly, she was hit by a charging police horse. As we said then, 'She put her body on the line.' If on the line, why not a wall?"
Author's note: see John Bennett portrait POR-045 in the final section of this book. Regarding the occupation see A History of Union Theological Seminary in New York, *Robert T. Handy, 1987, pp 273-82.*

Refectory with 13 portraits (7 in view), January 2012

"...Union is not a Black and White space..."

Rev. Dr. Eboni Marshall Turman, Womanist scholar: "I was speaking recently at the plenary of The Future of Liberation Theology conference held in the Social Hall. There had been much discussion at the conference about avoiding a Black and White binary that silences Latino, Asian, Queer, and others voices. I felt compelled to point out that Union is not a Black and White space. It is a White space and that it was so important not to lose sight of Black oppression in the process of making room for more diverse voices.

I noted that the portraits in the Social Hall underline the normative White historical narrative. It seems to me there is a disconnect between the ethos of Union and the décor, particularly as represented in those paintings. Who is remembered, honored? What would it mean to envisage different kinds of portraits? These current portraits raise such questions to the inquiring eye, but otherwise they confirm the status quo that this is a space of White power, authority, and male superiority."

"...the large mirror in the Social Hall..."

Elizabeth Bukey, MDiv student: "For me, the large mirror in the Social Hall is a way that I put myself into the story. The portraits may all be of unknown middle-aged white men, but when I stand in front of the mirror, there's also now an image of a queer young white woman hanging on the wall. When my classmates fill the room, the reflections of a bisexual black woman, a genderqueer activist, and a Dominican grandmother might join the portraits in fleshing out what Union Theological Seminary looks like."

"...'They don't look like you'..."

Serene Jones, President, Union Theological Seminary: "I'd only been here a month or so when my daughter, Charis, had five of her 12-year-old friends visiting from New Haven, where we used to live. I was showing them around the Seminary and when we came to the Social Hall they bounded in, still in their soccer uniforms after a game in Riverside Park. After just a few seconds, several of them stopped in their tracks to look at the portraits.

They looked at them carefully and then they looked at me. One of them remarked: 'They don't look like you.' Others agreed. It was a moment of recognition and cognitive dissonance: they knew I was the president, and they knew that these portraits were images of past leaders, but they couldn't see a resemblance. I thought, that's right. I don't look like them. That moment said so much to me about

Social Hall with 6 portraits (2 in view), January 2012

the absence of women's leadership, about justice and about social change."

"...portraits on one side and mirrors on the other..."

Christopher Morse, Dietrich Bonhoeffer Professor of Theology & Ethics: "A couple of things come to mind when you ask me about the portraits. In the Social Hall you have portraits on one side and mirrors on the other. You look at the portraits and you see yourself in the mirror. These mirrors are reflective of Union's attitude that everyone is valued and deserves to be in the picture.

Another thing is that Union has tended to hang portraits of Presidents of the Board and Faculty. So some of the most famous professors are not represented among the portraits.

As part of the orientation when I arrived in 1967, we were given a tour and shown various architectural features of the buildings, like the engravings. I think this was helpful in immediately understanding the integration of art and spirituality within the architecture. And we were given copies of the pamphlet, *Education Through Stone and Glass.*" *Author's note: narratives from this pamphlet (Daniel J. Fleming, ~1948) are quoted in the Catalog in the final section of this book.*

"...the distinguished past of the Seminary..."

Norman D. Stanton, Alum '64; VP for Seminary Relations, 1976–81: "For me, the portraits symbolize the distinguished past of the Seminary and I respect them. During the time I was VP it seemed there was an attack on the portraits and I think several were stolen and as far as I know they were not recovered. This saddened me and I suppose angered me a bit at the time.

The other thing I wanted to say is I think the portraits represent a very small part of Union's distinguished past. Many very important professors are not included in this collection. It seems to me there is a randomness in whose images we see on the walls."

"...the portraits as portrait of the collective..."

Ted Kerr, artist-in-residence 2011 and current intern at the Institute of Art, Religion, & Social Justice: "When asked why they work collectively, the art trio General Idea said it was because it 'freed us from the tyranny of the myth of the individual genius.' Of late, I like to look at the portraits with this idea in mind. I like to see them as a stand-in for everything that is not in the portrait, and as time capsules of Union. We see who is valued by the Union elite, gain a sense of different period's fashion, and get a glimpse into some of the characters that (for good or bad) shaped this school. Adding to this information is the state that the portraits are currently in. They are artifacts of Union's culture, as well as art objects. We can ask at least two questions when looking at them: how did they come to be? And how did they come to be in such a state? With these questions in mind, they become less oppressive for me. I become less angry about the ways in which power works, and feel more a part of the collective potential of Union. I think in seeing the portraits as a portrait of the collective we can begin to imagine more innovative and holistic ways of honoring our past."

Self-portrait as a Seminarian

Nicolas Dumit Estevez, MA student: "There is a portrait on the second floor between two classrooms [group portrait of Union faculty 1998–99 by Abdelilah Ennasses]. It may be a drawing. It has many faces in it. When at Union, I am always so busy rushing to class. Always trying to read one more sentence before presenting a reflection to a group of classmates and thinking about the thousand and one papers I have to write for almost every single course. And so, I often look at the many faces in this portrait, but I never stop to learn who these people really are or what they mean to the school. Nevertheless, the portrait I am referring to speaks of the two years I have spent at the Seminary, since the faces in it represent the part of me that I have missed in the midst of rushing up and down the stairs, or taking the elevator to the Pit. This portrait with the many faces operates as the image in my bathroom mirror I fail to pay attention to in the mornings, when trying to leave the house for a meeting with one of my three advisors. Next time I come to Union I will remember to bring disposable Bic razors, a box of Rite Aid unwaxed dental floss, and Aveeno cream, and to care for each one of the faces in the portrait with the many faces. I will make sure to take as long as needed."

"...There are very few women represented ..."

Barbara Lundblad, Professor of Preaching: "In the first floor Administration hall, there was a portrait of James Washington, a beloved former Union professor. It was painted by Abdelilah Ennasses, a contemporary artist who ran the bookstore and taught painting classes at Union. It had lots of blue and was almost abstract. There was some disagreement about whether or not it should be there because it was so unlike the other works. It disappeared within the past few years.

Across from the portrait of Charles Henry in the McGiffert lobby, I remember there was a portrait of another long-time building attendant, Alfred McMillan. I noticed it's gone now.

There are very few women represented among the portraits at Union. When I was a student at Yale Divinity School (YDS), there were no portraits of women. So a bunch of us got together, raised money and had Joan Forsberg's portrait done. Believe me this was no easy task! Since then, two others have been added: Letty Russell and Margaret Farley. So now there are three hanging in the midst of the male professors. I must say that I celebrate with joy every time I walk into the Common Room at YDS and see these three beloved women professors smiling at me."

"...how Union sees itself..."

Jeremy Kirk, PhD candidate in Social Ethics: "In my six years at Union, I have only heard the portraits mentioned when students are critiquing them. These critiques have to do with how Union sees itself as an innovator and hub of progressive religion. The place is branded as progressive and diverse, and we see this to some extent in the student population, yet not in the portraits. So the lack of respect people have towards the portraits can be seen as a manifestation of the tension between what is represented within them and who we claim to be as an institution and community.

There is no doubt in my mind that the people represented in the portraits were admirable and played an important role in our institution's history. However, they do not make up the school's entire history, or even its most significant history. Students would likely be more interested in the portraits that are hanging currently if they were joined by renderings of other significant members of Union's history such as Delores Williams, Beverly Harrison, James Washington, James Forbes and others."

"... it doesn't do him justice..."

Rev. Dr. James A. Forbes Jr., Harry Emerson Fosdick Distinguished Professor: "So you're the artist-in-residence and you're paying attention to the portraits. Do you know the one of Rev. James Robinson? He was one of my teachers. He was a great man. When I look at that portrait I feel it doesn't do him justice, it doesn't capture him very well. He was sharp and he seems to be looking off into the distance in that painting. He was someone who was right there with you when you were in his presence."

"...face-down..."

Leah Rousmaniere, Development Office: "I rescued this little painting (Thomas McAuley, first President of Union, 1836–1840, by Daniel P. Huntington) that was patiently awaiting discovery face-down on top of a forgotten file cabinet for a number of years. I kept it in my office for safekeeping some months while arrangements were made for a more suitable place, and enjoyed McAuley's amiable company in the meanwhile."

"...chairs that caused the damage..."

Troy Messenger, Director of Worship: "About twelve years ago a group of students lead by Elizabeth Schell, were looking for a place in the building to make art and suggested clearing out a basement storage room (now Columbia University property). In the process, we found a number of portraits propped up against the walls with chairs against them. I think it's the chairs that caused the damage. Not in a malicious way, but in an 'Oh, here's some space where we can put these chairs' way. I looked into having them wrapped and after that they were housed on the sixth and then eighth floor of Chapel Tower where you found them."

"…a living place…"

Michael Orzechowski, Director of Housing: "This isn't a museum, it's a living place, an organism. We invite the community, many kinds of people, to use our spaces and it's exciting that we're able to do that, to be integral to the neighborhood. We try to be as open as we can. On Sundays there are four congregations meeting simultaneously in various parts of the complex including the Eritrean Orthodox group in the Social Hall and the Korean United Methodist Church in James Chapel. And then there are the weddings and film shoots that help to sustain our operations, along with a wide range of mainly non-profit conferences. And the portraits, usually perceived as these white men looking down on them, are dealt with in one way or another, usually ignored and sometimes moved."

"…You can reflect on a ghost, but not on a beacon…"

Dorit Cypis, artist: "I think these portraits can be seen as beacons or as ghosts. If you take that iconic authority away from the object, it's the ghosts of the people represented that remain. Beacons are more like the sun with rays throwing out projected power. A ghost is a shadow, like memory. You can reflect on a ghost, but not on a beacon.

It seems to me this project is borrowing from the public address of the painted portraits and transferring it to the viewers, the subject of the portrait's gaze. It's channeling a dialogue between the silent aesthetic authority of the characters on canvas and the viewers, creating opportunity for multiple voices and perspectives. It's like bringing them down to the ground in order to have a dialogue with their peers."

"…waves of iconoclasm…"

Sergey Trostyanskiy, PhD candidate in Church History: "Two things that have always been unsettled in Christianity are prayer and art. There have been waves of anti-image sentiment throughout Church history dating back to the eighth century iconoclastic controversy resulting in the Triumph of Orthodoxy, which restored the use of images. Perhaps the portraits are casualties of this unstable relationship to images and the imitative arts."

CATALOG

01 *POR-062*

Dirck Cornelius Lansing DD 1785–1857
Professor of Sacred Rhetoric and Pastoral Theology, Auburn 1821–1826
Artist: Unknown
45 x 38
One of the first three professors at Auburn Theological Seminary

02 *POR-002*

Thomas McAuley DD LLD 1778–1862
Professor 1836-1840; President 1836-1840; Director 1836–1845
Artist: Daniel P. Huntington
16.75 x 15.5
First President of Union

03 *POR-063*

James Roosevelt 1760–1847
Benefactor
Artist: Unknown
42 x 38
Great-grandfather of President Franklin D. Roosevelt

04 *POR-036*

Rev. Henry White DD 1800–1850
Professor of Systematic Theology 1836–1850
Artist: Unknown
46.5 x 37

05 *POR-018*

William M. Halstead
Founder & Treasurer 1836–1851
Artist: Unknown
42.25 x 35.5

06 *POR-021*

Rev. Samuel Washburn
Artist: Unknown
40.5 x 30.5
In 1850 Mrs. Jacob Bell endowed the Washburn professorship of Church History
in memory of her brother, a Baltimore pastor.

07 *POR-048*

Rev Henry Mills DD 1786–1867
Professor Biblical Criticism, Auburn 1821–1854; Professor Emeritus 1854-1867
Artist: Unknown
48 x 38

08 *POR-033*

Rev. Edward Robinson DD LLD 1794–1863
Professor of Sacred Literature 1837–1863
Artist: Unknown
36 x 29

09 *POR-001*

Richard Townley Haines 1795–1870
Director 1836–1870; President of the Board 1840–1870; Union Founder
Artist: Unknown
Oil on board
36 x 29
Haines was a prominent merchant in New York who was a staunch supporter of the founding of the Seminary and present at some of the first meetings to establish Union.

10 *POR-004*

Fisher Howe
Director 1836–1871
Artist: Unknown
37 x 32.5

11 *POR-058*

Samuel Hanson Cox DD LLD 1793–1880
Professor, Auburn 1835–1837; Director UTS 1837–1873; President, Board of Directors 1840
Artist: Chas Peterson (reproduction, 1895)
43 x 38

12 *POR-024*

Jonathan Bailey Condit DD 1808–1876
Professor of Sacred Rhetoric and Pastoral Theology, Auburn 1854–1876
Artist: Unknown
30 x 25

13 *POR-014*

James Brown 1791–1877
Benefactor
Artist: Unknown
~63 x 49
James Brown was a close friend of Union President William Adams [see 15 and 16] and was "Union's largest contributor of the period. Long after Brown had established the famous banking firm of Brown Bothers & Co., a terrible tragedy had touched his family: lost at sea were a son, two daughters, a daughter-in-law,

and two grandchildren, with two nurses. His religious life was deepened by the experience, and his interest in Union, which was near his home, increased. His many gifts to the institution were crowned in 1873 with $300,000 for enlarging the endowments for the professorships so that they could produce sums adequate for the times.

A History of Union Theological Seminary in New York, Robert T. Handy, 1987

14 POR-010

Reverend Henry Boynton Smith DD LLD 1815–1877
Professor of Church History 1850–1854, Systematic Theology 1854–1874, and Apologetics 1874–1877
Artist: Unknown
42.25 x 37.5

15 POR-012

Rev. William Adams DD LLD
Professor of Sacred Rhetoric 1873–1880; President of the Faculty 1873–1880; Union Founder
Artist: Unknown
37.75 x 34.5
Presented by Governor Edwin D. Morgan

16 POR-056

Rev. William Adams DD LLD
Professor of Sacred Rhetoric 1873–1880; President of the Faculty 1873–1880; Union Founder
Artist: Unknown
63 x 55
Grandfather of William Adams Brown

17 POR-031

Rev. Roswell Dwight Hitchcock 1817–1887
President 1880–1887; Professor of Ecclesiastical History 1855–1887
Artist: Unknown
60 x 42

18 POR-019

Ransom Bethune Welch DD LLD 1824–1890
Professor & Chair Christian Theology, Auburn 1876–1890
Artist: Réal del Sarte
Conté crayon on paper-covered board
39.5 x 34.5
Welch Memorial Hall (built 1894), one of the few buildings remaining in Auburn NY after Auburn Theological Seminary moved to Union, is a national historic landmark.

19 POR-054

Rev. Philip Schaff DD LLD 1819-1893
Professor of Theological Encyclopedia & Symbolics 1870-1873; Professor of Hebrew & Cognate Languages 1873-1874; Professor of Sacred Literature 1874-1887; Professor of Church History 1887-1893
Artist: Unknown
40 x 27

Samuel Miles Hopkins DD
Professor of Ecclesiastical History and Church Polity 1847–1901
Artist: Chas Petersen (1894)
40 x 35

20 POR-064

Rev. John Hopkins Worcester DD 1845-1893
Professor of Systematic Theology 1891–1893
Artist: Hugo Breul (1896)
38 x 32.5

21 POR-037

Charles Butler LLD
Founder & Director 1836–1897; Vice President 1840–1870; President of the
Board 1870-1897; Benefactor
Artist: William M. J. Rice
49.75 x 40

22 POR-028

George Lewis Prentiss 1816–1903
Professor of Pastoral Theology, Church Polity & Mission Work 1873–1897;
Professor Emeritus 1897-1903
Artist: Unknown
30 x 25

23 POR-061

Rev. Henry M. Booth DD LLD 1843–1899
First President, Auburn 1893-1899
Artist: J. Colin Forbes
69.5 x 47

24 POR-039

Rev. Ezra Abel Huntington DD LLD
Professor, Auburn 1854–1893; Professor of Biblical Criticism 1854–1901
Artist: Unknown
~37 x 29

25 POR-017

Rev. Thomas Samuel Hastings DD LLD LHD 1827–1911
Director 1864–1881 and 1887–1897; President of Faculty 1887–1897;
Professor of Sacred Rhetoric 1881-1904
Artist: Unknown
Oil on board
36.5 x 30.75

26 POR-029

"...After two refusals he finally yielded and accepted the Presidency in 1888. Here he showed fitness for administration. And yet with all the new responsibilities there was no less attention to his teaching in Homiletics and Pastoral Theology. During the trying years of controversy (1891-93) when the Seminary was fighting for the ecclesiastical rights of its faculty and for the ecclesiastical independence of the Seminary, Dr. Hastings' tact, good temper and great ability made all his colleagues grateful for his leadership."

Education through Stone and Glass, Daniel J. Fleming, ~1948, p. 47

27 POR-042

Rev. Thomas Samuel Hastings DD LLD LHD 1827-1911
Director 1864-1881 and 1887-1897; President of Faculty 1887-1897; Professor
of Sacred Rhetoric 1881-1904
Artist: Unknown
~60 x 48.5

28 POR-020

Timothy Grenville Darling DD
Professor of Sacred Rhetoric & Pastoral Theology 1887–1890 and
Christian Theology, Auburn 1890–1906
Artist: Unknown
40 x 35

29 POR-041

Charles Cuthbert Hall DD LLD 1852–1908
Director 1883-1908; Professor 1897–1908; President of the Faculty 1897–1908
Artist: Unknown
~70 x 54
"...Those who knew him were impressed by Dr. Hall's deep reverence for the
personality of every student. His interest in men as individuals was one of his
marked characteristics, symbolized by the open door which Dr. Hall ordered to
be cut through between the dormitory at the Park Avenue site and the adjoining
President's residence – a realization of the desire of the founders and early
Directors that faculty and students should form a little Christian community. He
was affectionately loved by the members of those classes which had studied
under him. Through the pastoral influence exerted by Dr. Hall in daily contact
with individual men and through the new social spirit fostered by his influence
there was a distinct deepening of the spiritual life within the student body."
Education through Stone and Glass, Daniel J. Fleming, ~1948, p. 50 – 51

30 POR-015

Morris Ketchum Jesup 1830–1908
Director 1883–1908; Vice President of the Board 1907–1908
Artist: Unknown
60 x 50.25
Mr. Jesup was a significant philanthropist with particular interest in aiding new
immigrants to the USA.

John Crosby Brown, LLD, 1838–1909
Director 1866–1909; Vice President 1883–1898; President of the Board
1898–1909
Artist: Unknown
~37 x 30
"...Mr. John Crosby Brown was not only a layman with wide business interests,
great financial skill, and a large place in the councils of men of influence, but
was a great molder of the Seminary, entering fully into the noble traditions of
his family's interest in it. For over forty years, first as a member and later as
President of the Board of Directors, he served this institution with devotion,
self-sacrifice, minute attention to all details, and constant care for the higher
interests of the Seminary. He entered with extraordinary clearness of insight
into the Seminary's historic aim of uniting breadth and freedom of thought to
loving and religious service in establishing God's Kingdom on earth. His life and
service, commemorated in the Memorial Tower, provide an inspiring example of
noble Christian influence on the part of a devoted layman."
Education through Stone and Glass, Daniel J. Fleming, ~1948 p. 44

31 POR-046

32 POR-013

Daniel Willis James, 1832–1907
Director 1867–1907; Vice President of the Board 1898–1907
Artist: Hubert Vos (1915?)
63 x 47.25
James Chapel is dedicated in his name.
"Through his portrait and especially though this memorial tablet [in a recess
on the north wall of the vestibule to James Chapel] the Seminary gratefully

acknowledges its great indebtedness to another layman. That Union now has connection with a great University community was largely due to his most generous gifts and foresight. It was he who gave the Seminary the two blocks, which compose the main portion of Union's present site. An almost equally great gift was made for the new building of 1910. In all his benefactions amounted to $1,900,000."

Education through Stone and Glass, Daniel J. Fleming, ~1948, p. 45

33 *POR-011*

Francis Brown PhD DD LLD D. Litt 1849–1916
Instructor in Biblical Philosophy 1879–1881; Associate Professor of Biblical Philosophy 1881–1890; Professor of Hebrew and the Cognate Languages 1890–1916; President of the Faculty 1908–1916; Director 1908–1916
Artist: Unknown
74.25 x 55.25
"Over the fireplace in the Social Hall is the portrait of Dr. Brown. From it, one catches the impression of a lofty and majestic figure...But he was the soul of modesty, was extraordinarily gentle, full of generosity and kindness, and quick to help when help was needed. On the other hand he was marked by a lion-hearted boldness, which was undaunted, as was shown in the vigorous part he played in the famous "Briggs controversy" of 1891–92."

Education through Stone and Glass, Daniel J. Fleming, ~1948, p. 51

34 *POR-030*

Charles Ripley Gillett DD LHD 1855–1948
Librarian 1883–1908; Secretary of Faculty 1898–1929; Dean of Students 1913–1929
Artist: Wilford S. Conrow 1880-1957
53.5 x 42

35 *POR-038*

Arthur Cushman McGiffert DD LLD 1861–1933
President of the Faculty 1917–1926; Director 1917–1926; Professor 1893–1928
Artist: Unknown
56.5 x 42
Dr. McGiffert's best-known publication is *A History of Christianity in the Apostolic Age* (1897). This book, by its independent criticism and departures from traditionalism, aroused the opposition of the General Assembly of the Presbyterian Church, though the charges brought against McGiffert were dismissed by the Presbytery of New York.
"Dr. McGiffert was a brilliant lecturer, presenting the results of his scholarly study in a way that fascinated students for a generation. As President he labored unsparingly on behalf of the Seminary, and gave substance to the vision of Union's mission as a school of sacred learning...Dr. McGiffert's character as a Christian gentleman, his exceptional gifts of intellect, his thorough scholarship, his fearlessness in inquiry, his unswerving devotion to the cause of truth, his passion to find and to face the fact, and the stimulus that went forth from him for the diligent study of the Church's heritage, continue to be an inspiration to all..."

Education through Stone and Glass, Daniel J. Fleming, ~1948, p. 49 - 50

36 *POR-027*

Rev. Charles Henry Parkhurst 1842–1933
Board of Directors 1881–1926
Artist: Paul King
40 x 32
Rev. Parkhurst took a public stand against social and political corruption in Tammany Hall and the New York Police Department, suggesting links with organized crime, and denouncing these criminal activities from the pulpit. Facing challenges to his claims, he hired a detective and personally went undercover to gather evidence. His work prompted a formal inquiry leading to the election of a reform mayor in 1894.

37 *POR-008*

Charles Ripley Gillett DD LHD 1855–1948
Librarian 1883-1908; Secretary of Faculty 1898–1929; Dean of Students
1913–1929
Artist: A. T. Shirley
23.25 x 19.25

38 *POR-009*

Charles Ripley Gillett DD LHD 1855-1948
Librarian 1883–1908; Secretary of Faculty 1898–1929; Dean of Students
1913–1929
Artist: A. T. Shirley
22 x 17.25

39 *POR-007*

Robert Curtis Ogden LLD LHD
Director 1897–1913; President of the Board 1909–1913
Artist: Hubert Vos 1855-1935 (1930)
57 x 47
Mr. Ogden was a prominent merchant and retired from the firm of John Wanamaker. He was a generous supporter of causes important to black people. He gave the Address of Presentation, Nov 28-29, 1910, the time of the formal dedication of the new buildings and the date chosen for the 75th anniversary.

40 *POR-026*

William Adams Brown 1865–1943
Professor of Church History 1892–1893; Professor of Systematic Theology
1893–1930; Research Professor In Applied Christianity 1930–1936
Artist: J.W. L. Forster 1850–1938
40.5 x 30
In 1904 Brown joined others like Charles Parkhurst in the fight against the corrupt political machine of Tammany Hall. Brown was also invited to join the Committee of Fourteen, a group that was formed to fight commercialized vice. They worked to end prostitution in the city by cutting off the supply of liquor, with the open participation of the liquor distributors themselves. Brown was also instrumental in the founding of Union Settlement in East Harlem. The settlement movement began in the 1880's as a way to improve the lives of people in poorer communities.

41 *POR-023*

Clarence Dickinson MA MusD
Instructor, School of Sacred Music 1912–1928; Associate Professor
1929–1945; Director, School of Sacred Music 1928–1945
Artist: Alice zur Cann Boscowitz 1875–1962 (1940)
40 x 34
Clarence Dickinson co-founded the School of Sacred Music at Union Theological Seminary with his wife, Dr. Helen Dickinson. The school had the distinction of being the first graduate level music program for men and women in the United States. Prior to its founding in 1928, those who wanted to pursue a graduate degree in sacred music were forced to travel to Europe. Dr. Dickinson—organist and choirmaster, composer, virtuoso, performer, author, lecturer, and teacher —worked in all his capacities to broaden appreciation of organ music and to improve the quality of church music.

42 *POR-022*

Helen (or Helena) Adell Dickinson MA PhD MusD 1875–1957
Lecturer, School of Sacred Music 1928–1953
Artist: Alice zur Cann Boscowitz 1875–1962 (1940)
40 x 34
Dr. Helen Adell Dickinson was the first woman to receive a PhD from Heidelberg University in Germany. She was a well-known lyricist, translator, art historian and author of three books. Together with her husband, Dr. Clarence Dickinson, she founded the Union School of Sacred Music and wrote hundreds of choral anthems for church choirs.

43 *POR-006*

Arthur Curtiss James Esq. 1867–1941
Director 1908–1941
Artist: Raymond P. R. Neilson NA
30 x 25
Arthur Curtiss James was the son of Daniel Willis James [see 32].
"Mr. Arthur Curtiss James continued his father's interest in the Seminary, and was a member of the Board of Directors until his death in 1941. With his mother he gave the beautiful Seminary Chapel as a memorial to his father. There followed, both from Mr. Arthur Curtiss James and from his mother, liberal gifts toward the expanded site across Claremont Avenue and towards such growing needs as the Gymnasium, McGiffert Hall, the Library, the Chapel organ and choir and the Seminary endowment. Thus the James family has been most helpfully connected with the Union Seminary for three quarters of a century; and the James Foundation of New York, set up by the will of Mr. Arthur Curtiss James continues to be a generous supporter of the Seminary."

Education through Stone and Glass, Daniel J. Fleming, ~1948, p. 47

44 *POR-049*

William Morgan Kingsley, 1863–1942
Director 1901–1942; Recorder 1901–1913; President of the Board 1913–1936
Artist: _____ R. Boynton
~37.75 x 32.5

45 *POR-032*

William Walker Rockwell STB STL PhD D Theol. 1874–1958
Assistant Director 1905–1917; Associate Professor 1917–1925; Librarian 1925–1942
Artist: Alice zur Cann Boscowitz 1875-1962
42 x 32

46 *POR-043*

Dr. Henry Sloane Coffin 1877–1954
Assistant and Associate Professor 1904–1926; Professor and President of Faculty 1926–1945
Artist: Gordon Aymar (copy of original)
37.5 x 29.5
Henry Sloane Coffin was a clergyman, author, and educator who led in the movement for liberal evangelicalism in Protestant churches. Coffin emphasized the application of Christianity to social problems. He also sought to improve the quality of theological education. He authored more than 20 books.
"Dr. Coffin…was for a generation the most widely recognized preacher of the gospel in the universities of the country. He was a leader in the liberal wing of Presbyterianism but also one of those whose thought contributed to healing the breach within the denomination…In recent years he has been particularly active in the negotiations looking toward a union between the Episcopal and Presbyterian Churches. Throughout his ministry he has been one of the most thoughtful and resourceful exponents of the application of the principles of the Christian faith to industrial and political affairs."

Education through Stone and Glass, Daniel J. Fleming, ~1948, p.45-46

47 *POR-059*

Dr. Henry Sloane Coffin 1877–1954
Assistant and Associate Professor 1904–1926; Professor and President of Faculty 1926–1945
Artist: Ernest L. Ipsen NA
56.5 x 42.5

48 *POR-040*

Harold H. Tryon
Member of the Faculty 1908–1947; Registrar 1924–1944; Secretary of the Faculty 1929–1944
Artist: Alice zur Cann Boscowitz 1875–1962
37 x 32.5

49 *POR-050*

Thatcher Magoun Brown 1876–1954
Director 1908–1954; Treasurer 1924–1936; President of the Board 1936–1947
Artist: Raymond P. R. Neilson (1947)
38 x 33

50 *POR-035*

Charles Henry
McGiffert Attendant 1913–1957
Artist: Mrs. Henry Pitney Van Dusen (Betty Bartholomew)
21 x 17.25
Mr. Henry continued his work at Union part-time until 1966, making 53 years of service.

51 *POR-003*

Benjamin Strong
Director 1933–1965; Treasurer 1936–1947; President of the Board 1947–1952; Chairman of the Board 1952–1961
Artist: Elmer Wesley Greene 1907–1964 (1961)
44 x 38

52 *POR-044*

Henry Pitney Van Dusen 1897–1975
President of the Faculty 1945–1963; Assistant & Associate Professor 1928–1936; Professor 1945–1963
Artist: Raymond P. R. Neilson 1881–1964
37 x 32.5
When Van Dusen graduated from Union, a conservative-minded judicial commission of the Presbyterian General Assembly challenged his ordination because he declined to affirm the literal Biblical account of the virgin birth.

The Union Faculty and Board of Directors in their final tributes claims that he enlarged not only the personal and physical resources of the Seminary, but above all, its spirit and its outreach. The Board of Directors saluted him as one of the first World Churchmen of the era and a leader in the ecumenical movement.

In 1975, Henry Pitney, along with his wife, Elizabeth (Betty), both members of the Euthanasia Society, took overdoses of sleeping pills to end their lives, due to increasingly poor health.

Rev. James H. Robinson DD 1907–1972
Pastor of Church of the Master and founder of Crossroads Africa
Artist: Margery A. Ryerson
53.5 x 41.5
Following his graduation from Union and ordination in 1938, Robinson became pastor of Harlem's Church of the Master. That year he established the Morningside Community Center, setting up a cooperative store and a credit union. He co-founded the African Academy of Arts and Research in 1943. After extensive tours including of Africa, he suggested that the church focus on sending doctors, engineers and other professionals, rather than missionaries. In 1958, Robinson's efforts coalesced with the establishment of Operation Crossroads Africa (OCA), which aimed to provide volunteer opportunities for

53 *POR-055*

students and professionals to help build infrastructure and improve education in impoverished African communities. This evolved into the Peace Corps.

In 1964, Robinson appeared before the House Committee on Un-American Activities to refute suspicions that he harbored communist sympathies. He denied ever being a communist, though he stated that before World War II, he had knowingly worked with communists who supported causes that he supported, such as civil rights.

54 POR-045

John Coleman Bennett 1902–1995
Systematic Theology & Philosophy of Religion 1927–1930; Professor of Christian Theology, Auburn 1930–1938; Professor of Christian Theology & Ethics, Union 1943–1970; Dean of the Faculty 1955–1963; President 1963–1970
Artist: Paul C. _____
49 x 40.5
Rev. Bennett was an American Protestant social ethicist and a leading Christian thinker in the twentieth century who applied ethical principles to urgent issues of modern society. He was the first holder of the Reinhold Niebuhr Professorship in Social Ethics at Union. His involvement in political and social issues extended to participation in the civil rights movement, protests against the war in Vietnam, opposition to the use of nuclear weapons, and, late in his life, advocacy of gay and lesbian rights within the church.

55 POR-052

Rosalind Everdell Havemeyer
Director 1965–1981; Chair, Board of Directors 1970–1975
Artist: Everett Raymond Kinstler (1983)
40.5 x 34.5
Benefactor and first Chairwoman of the Board. She helped spearhead the renovation of James Chapel.

56 POR-047

Anne Hale Johnson
Chair, Board of Directors 1995–2004
Artist: (2004)
~42 x 30.5
Under her leadership, the Seminary progressed from some of the most severe financial crises in its history…On her watch, a new Master of Divinity curriculum and a reconfigured PhD program were put into place.

57 POR-051

Joseph C. Hough
President 1999–2008
Artist: Istvan Nyikos
45.75 x 37.5
Joseph C. Hough was highly proficient fund-raiser. He played a major role in establishing the Luce and Nielsen Chairs. He was also instrumental in securing full funding for two existing chairs: The Reinhold Niebuhr Chair in Social Ethics and The Paul Tillich Chair of Theology, World Religions, and Culture.

58 POR-053

Donald W. Shriver
President 1975–1991
Artist: James Pollard (2009)
49 x 38
Professor Shriver is an international voice in examining ethical issues related to race relations, youth, business, politics and medicine and author of thirteen books on ethics. He has also engaged in Jewish-Christian dialogue in several countries. He was a fellow of the American Academy in Berlin and visiting senior scholar of the Institute for Justice and Reconciliation in Cape Town, South Africa.

Unidentified
Artist: Samuel Lawrence (1859)
Chalk on paper, under glass
35.25 x 29.5

59 *POR-025*

Unidentified
Artist: Unknown
36 x 30.75

60 *POR-057*

Unidentified
Artist: Unknown
Oil pastel on paper, under glass
41.5 x 34.5

61 *POR-005*

Unidentified
Artist: Unknown
38 x 29.5
The subject of this portrait bears a resemblance to a younger photograph of
Rev. James Richards, Professor of Christian Theology, Auburn 1823–1843

62 *POR-034*

Unidentified
Artist: Martin D. Hardin
~46 x 35

63 *POR-016*

Missing Portraits

Thomas McAuley DD LLD (1778–1862)*; Matthew Larue Perrine DD (1777–1836); Joel Parker DD (1799–1873); Rev. James Richards DD (1767–1843); Anson Green Phelps, Jr. (1818–?); Samuel Hanson Cox DD LLD (1793–1880)*; Rev. Edwin Hall DD (1802–1877); Ezra Munson Kingsley (1817–1903); Rev. George Black Stewart DD STD LLD (1854–1932); Rev. Harry Lathrop Reed DD STD (1867–1964); Eugene William Lyman STD DD (1872–1948); Alfred McMillan, McGiffert Attendant, 1923–1958; James M. Washington (1948–1997).
According to our lists these subjects should have two portraits; only one of each has been found.

All portraits are oil on canvas unless otherwise noted. '~' indicates estimated measurement or date. Information in this Catalog was compiled from: *Lists of Union Paintings, Plaques and Memorials* (1951, 1966 and 1973); *A History of Union Theological Seminary in New York*, Robert T. Handy; *Education Through Stone and Glass*, Daniel J. Fleming; Burke Library Archives; direct examination (nameplates, labels, writing on the portraits); Internet sources (Union website, Wikipedia, art, history, biographical and genealogy sites, online obituaries and news items); and professional consultants (archivists, conservators, art specialists). It is not considered a complete catalog, but is accurate to the best of our ability within the scope of this project. An online read-only version entitled *Non-Photographic Portraits at Union Theological Seminary 2012* is available on the Union website.